# contents

# acknowledgements

Everything in this book has been based on fieldwork and research done between 1971 and 1981 and without the co-operation of the players themselves both young and old, this work would not have been possible. In particular, I must thank Seamus Tansey, Marcus Walsh, John McInerney, Dinny Considine, J. P. Downes, Roundy Lawlor, Mick Sheehy, Sonny Cannafin, Pat Flynn, Packie Maloney, Mel Mercier, John McDonagh, Martin O'Connor, Maurice Lennon and Tommy Hayes. Apart from these and other musicians, I was assisted in my fieldwork in Co. Clare by Muiris O'Rocháin and Michael Roberts, and the greater part of my video recordings would not have been possible without the professional guidance and expert advice of Tony Perrot of the Audio-Visual Department of University College, Cork. This research was funded in part by the Faculty of Arts Research Fund Committee of University College, Cork and the necessary quietness and stability for writing was provided by the Benedictine Community of Glenstal Abbey.

Dr. John Baily and Professor John Blacking have influenced this and other writings through their stimulating courses and seminars at Queens University, Belfast, and Keith Howard, a student of Korean drumming, has made valuable comments on my approach in this case.

I am also indebted to the Secretarial Centre of University College, Cork, and to John O'Sullivan of the National Museum of Ireland for providing photographs of Bodhráns in the museum's collection. A particular word of thanks to Martin Walton for his invitation to write this book, especially for his patience in the final stages. Finally, my wife Nóirín Ní Riain assisted me right throughout the work, in particular with some of the more important field trips in the early seventies.

# introduction

In the past, bodhrán players in Ireland acquired their skill by being in an environment where bodhrán playing was a natural activity associated with certain rituals in the folk-year. Since the 1950s, the instrument has spread from a rural to an urban setting, from amateur to professional status, from being exclusively male to including female performers, from an outdoor to an indoor performance situation, from having the combined function of skin tray (or sieve) and percussion instrument to being exclusively the latter, and from being tied to such folk-rituals as 'hunting the wren' on St. Stephen's Day (December 26) to being a freely-used instrument.

Dramatic changes in playing-styles have resulted from all of this and these stylistic changes are both disturbing and exciting. On the one hand there is the inevitable decay of regional styles with the resultant loss of local techniques and approaches, and on the other, the increase in technical complexity along with an imaginative use of the instrument in new situations. At the present time, however, both the old and the new styles exist alongside one another and it is this duality of existence which makes the bodhrán such a dynamic instrument.

Unlike the other traditional instruments, no learning structure has evolved in recent years for those who wish to play the bodhrán. The aspiring player has been expected to battle with the beginners problems himself One of the dangers inherent in any tutor, however, is that it might contribute to a lack of individuality by favouring a particular style of playing to the exclusion of other styles. Since it is not possible for most people to consider following a particular regional style only, this increases the importance of being aware of the existence of the principal styles for the individual to achieve the best personal synthesis.

## THE BODHRAN TUTOR

## ISBN 1 85720 000 4

© Waltons Musical Instrument Galleries, 1984, 2-5 North Frederick Street, Dublin 1, Telephone: 8747805
Printed in Ireland by Betaprint, Dublin

# 1. the BODHRÁN AN IRISH FRAME DRUM

From the point of view of shape, drums fall into three categories:

1) Tubular drums in which the body is a tube
2) Kettledrums in which the body is a vessel
3) Frame-drums in which a frame is used in place of a body

It is into this final category of frame drums that the bodhrán fits. This kind of drum is found in many cultures, and interesting comparisons can be made by viewing the accompanying illustrations of European frame drums.

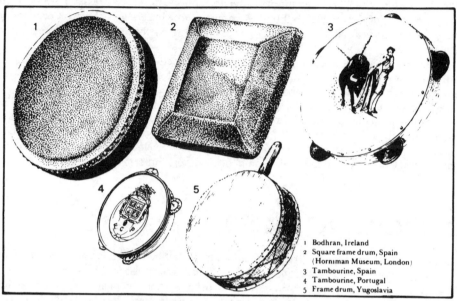

1 Bodhran, Ireland
2 Square frame drum, Spain
  (Horniman Museum, London)
3 Tambourine, Spain
4 Tambourine, Portugal
5 Frame drum, Yugoslavia

Illustration I  European frame drums

Some of these drums are single-headed like the bodhrán; others are double-headed with a skin at each end. The bodhrán skin is attached to the frame by nailing, though there is a drum in the National Museum of Ireland which has the skin lapped completely around the frame and tucked in under itself. The bodhrán is not a tuned drum even though the player needs to be sensitive to the general skin tension of his instrument. Many frame drums have jingles attached to the rim like the popular tambourine, and some varieties of bodhrán have these jingles also.

Drums are considered to have magical and ritual significance in many cultures. At least three occasions in the Irish 'folk-year'' involved procession rituals and included the use of the bodhrán: Lá le Bríde (St. Brighid's Day, February 1), Lá Bealtaine (May Day, May 1) and Lá le Stíofáin (St. Stephen's Day, December 26). Its strongest links seem to have been with 'hunting the wren' on St. Stephen's Day and it is in this context that it survived most strongly into the 20th century.

The bodhrán is a single-headed frame drum, sometimes with jingles inset in the rim or frame. These might range from carefully made circular tin discs to flattened beer-bottle caps. Either the bare hand or a stick may be used in playing. The skin is tacked on to the frame and a criss-cross system of cord, sticks or wire provides the means of holding the instrument while in a standing position. This holding method may also be used while sitting, but frequently the left hand is placed on top of the frame and the instrument is rested on the knee. The left hand is used to hold the bodhrán and the right hand to play, unless the player is left-handed when the situation is, of course, reversed. The skin may be that of a goat, deer, greyhound, ass-foal, or even of a horse provided the section under the saddle is that cut for the bodhrán.

Illustration 2A   The Bodhrán  (Copyright Dept. of Irish Folklore U.C.D.
Photos by Caoimhín Ó Danachair 1946)

Illustration 2B   Two bodhráns in the National Museum of Ireland with the skin wrapped around the rim and tucked under the rim on the inside. There is straw padding between the skin and the rim.

There is an interesting overlap between the bodhrán as a percussion instrument and its use as a skin tray or sieve. When used in the latter manner, it received a variety of names such as bodhrán, dallán, weight or wecht, depending on the area where it was found. It is also quite common to find that bodhrán rims are, in fact, re-used sieve rims among some of the older makers.

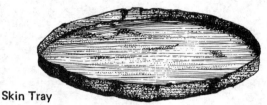

Illustration 3    Skin Tray

The word 'bodhrán' (pronounced — Bough—rawn) appears to be derived from the word *bodhar* meaning 'deaf' and 'dull-sounding' and it seems therefore that the name of the instrument was suggested by its sound. In Kerry, however, it is referred to as a 'tambourine' and the player as a 'tambourine tipper'. The stick used for playing is also referred to as a 'tipper'. In Co. Sligo, the player is referred to as a 'bodhrán stricker'. The 'tipper' or stick is about 8" or 9" in length on average, and may be carved from ash, holly, hickory or other wood. Depending on the style of playing, the stick may have a knob at both ends, or at one end only. A strip of leather may be fastened to the centre of the stick to form a holding loop but this is the exception rather than the rule. A small stick of about 4" with a leather loop at one end and a carved knob at the other is sometimes found, again depending on the style used.

Illustration 4    The stick or 'tipper'

# 2. playing the Bodhrán

### FOLLOWING THE TUNE

In European art-music, percussion instruments are used to mark the principal accents in a piece of music or occasionally to highlight certain misplaced accents or syncopations.

In Jazz, percussion is most frequently used to form a rhythmic 'base' against which the instrumental player can syncopate. Jazz percussion is also used to highlight some misplaced accents and syncopations even while the 'base' is continued. In *tabla* playing in Indian classical music, the complex rhythmic patterns are sometimes brought into synchronisation with the rhythm of the melodic line it is accompanying.

Experienced bodhrán players insist that the correct method of playing the bodhrán is to 'follow the tune' as an ideal. In practice, this is never done in an exact computerised fashion with every triplet or ornament accompanied by some appropriate bodhrán stroke. It can often be taken as referring to the phrasing of the tune as much as to its rhythm. The flute is the classic instrument for bodhrán accompaniment and when breathing points are followed by the bodhrán player, an added impetus or 'lift' is given to the music  (Example 1)

The bodhrán player must not only be competent technically, but must also understand the music he is accompanying. To know the tune itself is an advantage, as also is a knowledge of the tune-player's style and of the possibilities of his instrument.

For the older traditional bodhrán player, all of these requirements were understood to be contained in the concept of 'following the tune'.

3

## THE DIFFERENT STYLES

From the point of view of technique, <u>there are three main styles of playing:</u>

1. using both ends of the stick
2. using only one end of the stick
3. using the bare hand

Within each of these styles there are subdivisions characterised by different methods of holding the stick; or, in the case of hand-playing, different hand shapes. Nevertheless, in the end, these three main divisions represent the essential differences of style.

There is no traditional terminology for these various approaches. We will refer to them, therefore, as follows:

1. the double-ended stick style
2. the single-ended stick style
3. the hand style

In all styles, the bodhrán itself is held the same way. Gripping the cross-cords or their equivalent at the open end of the instrument with the left hand (assuming one is right-handed).

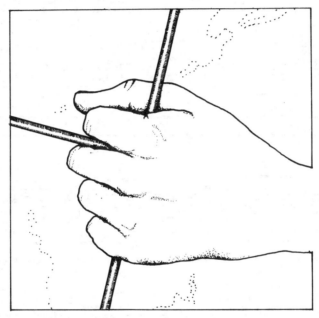

Illustration 5    Holding the Bodhrán

## THE DOUBLE—ENDED STICK STYLE

The most widely accepted method of holding the stick within this style is as follows. Hold it as if you were holding a pen, but more towards the middle than the writing end. Now turning your hand at the wrist move the stick around towards you until the lower knob (the 'writing end') is, more or less, facing towards your chest. Your hand will now be about right-angles to the bodhrán skin. By swivelling your hand from the elbow, as if you were turning a doorknob, you will be able to strike the skin with the stick-end nearest your body. Each swivel of the wrist produces a single beat — either a down-beat (away from the body) or an up-beat (in towards the body). A loose wrist will make the movement less rigid and more natural. It is essential at this stage to ensure that the other end of the stick (the 'top of the pen') does not come into contact with the drumskin. In order to achieve this, you will find that the stick will need to be at an angle to the skin.

4

Ex. 1    An extract from a transcription of 'The Navvy on the Line', a reel on flute with
bodhrán accompaniment by Seamus Tansey. Recorded in 1980.

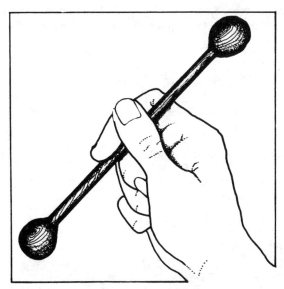

Illustration 6    Holding the stick (double-ended stick style)

Initially the feeling is one of awkwardness and you may wonder why a more 'natural' method is not adopted, with the hand in its normal position and with both ends of the stick hitting the skin alternately (the instinctive approach of most beginners and of children). Rest assured, however, that there is a very special reason for the traditional bodhrán hand-position which becomes obvious as you progress.

*This hand-position, used in all styles, is the secret to correct and effective bodhrán-playing.* It is the physical reason why playing the bodhrán is not the same as playing the medieval tabor, the Eskimo carribou-drum or the Turkish *tar* (all of which are frame drums of similar construction to the bodhrán).

An alternative less common method of holding the stick is to insert the third finger into a leather loop fastened to the centre. The stick is then held between the third finger and the second and fourth fingers.

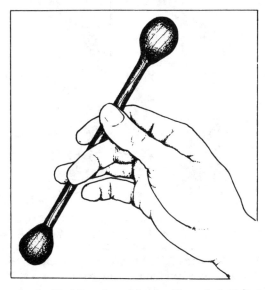

Illustration 7    A second method of holding the stick (double-ended stick style)

You are now ready for your first practising session. Continue to swivel the stick to produce a beat with each up and down stroke. Begin slowly and try to maintain a regular rhythm like the ticking of a clock.

Example 2

The symbols being used here above the notes should be interpreted in the following manner:

⊓ = down-stroke
V = up-stroke

Illustration 8a    Down-stroke

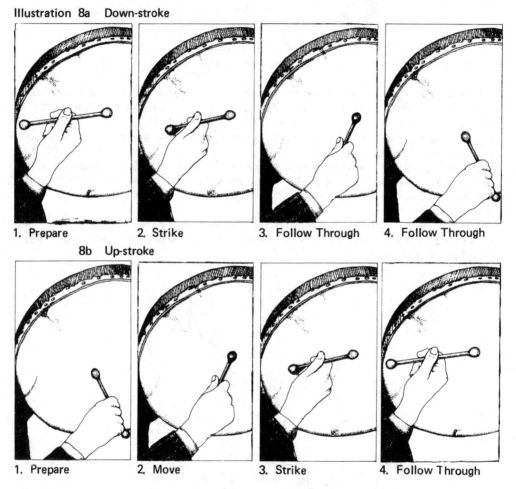

1. Prepare    2. Strike    3. Follow Through    4. Follow Through

8b    Up-stroke

1. Prepare    2. Move    3. Strike    4. Follow Through

Remember, only one end of the stick is being used at this stage. Be careful to follow-through with each stroke i.e. do not stop the stick moving at the point of impact. The moment of contact between stick and skin should be as brief as possible. Avoid 'rubbing' the stick on the skin by allowing the stick-end to rebound off the skin. A light brisk rapid stroke should be aimed at. As you begin to relax and your hand movement becomes less stiff, certain beats will begin to stand out above others.

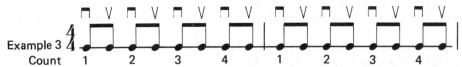

Example 3

Count    1      2      3      4      1      2      3      4

These accented beats should always be on down-strokes (⊓). In the above example you might try counting aloud and laying an emphasis on the number *one* by striking the down-stroke on that number more forcefully. This is best achieved by bringing back your arm at the elbow without losing the regularity of the rhythm.

From this point on in the book, those who do not read music should not be dismayed at the increasing use of musical examples. By reading the text carefully and by following the signs over the music showing up and down beats, it will be possible to understand what is being said.

For those who do read music, remember that the advantage this gives you should be offset against the danger of relying too heavily on the printed note and of your rhythms sounding 'literate' rather than 'aural'. Bodhrán players have never had any need or use for notation of any kind and the only reason it is being used here is to help bridge the gap between author and reader.

## A NOTE FOR MUSIC READERS

Since Irish traditional music is a non-literate tradition it fits uneasily into staff-notation, even though this is increasingly playing a subservient role in tune transmission and storage for traditional musicians. The greatest difficulty and the one which concerns us here is that of rhythm. The regular divisions of the written notes into halves and quarters evolved for a kind of music other than the traditional music of Ireland. The common mistake made by people attempting to play traditional music from notation is to read what they see. This invariably produces stodgy rhythms even when dealing with the best transcription. The reason for this is that the rhythms of Irish traditional dance music are 'swing' rhythms. In terms of notation it might be explained by the following.

The rhythm of a reel is usually shown as:

Example 4    

but traditional players give a longer durational value to the first of each group of two quavers. The exact value will vary from style to style and from player to player.

Writing it like this is no solution either:

Example 5    

Here the duration of the first quaver of each group is too long.

Writing it as follows is more likely to produce the required effect:

Example 6

This however could more effectively be written in $\frac{12}{8}$ time:

Example 7     Even this, however, is not satisfactory on account of the variability of the 'swing' ingredient. All of this goes to show how inadequate notation can be when dealing with an oral-tradition music and is dealt with here in order to impress upon the reader the danger of relying too heavily on the eye and not sufficiently on the ear.

The best solution is to retain the original 'even quavers' notation in alla-breve time, and to assume that the reader is by now an informed one, capable of making the necessary adjustments in sound. The more familiar we are with Irish traditional music generally, the more effective our adjustments will be, and that familiarity can only be achieved through consistent listening to the music, preferably in a live situation although recordings can be very useful for practising. Similar problems arise in all the other tune types including those in compound time such as the various forms of jigs.

After all of that, those who cannot read music are probably feeling thankful that even if they have something to learn, they have nothing to unlearn!

## RANDOM PLAY

The principle of random play in music is that every instrument lends itself to certain rhythmic, melodic or harmonic patterns. These are determined by the construction of the instrument itself (which in turn is affected by the musical demands of the musician) interacting with the accepted method of playing (holding the instrument etc). In the case of the bodhrán, once the secret of the hand position has been unfolded and a basic facility mastered, then the player finds that certain rhythms happen almost by accident. 'Going with' the instrument is as important at this stage as going against it will be when you advance in technical ability.

As you play an even pattern of beats, you may find that certain movements of the stick do not make contact with the skin as intended and as a result produce a 'silent beat'. In other words, you go through the movement as if you were making a sound, but you make none. You will learn to control this by deliberately not hitting the skin on certain selected up-strokes.

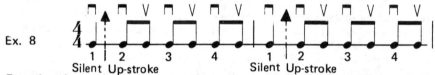

Ex. 8

Even though two down-strokes are shown here as following one another, there is a *silent* up-stroke in between. Your wrist should be making the same movements as if you were producing Example 3.

In practising the following examples, moving into ¢ time will help you get the right swing. For those who do not understand time-signatures, I have changed the counting system to convey the feeling of cycles of two beats rather than four. Counting aloud as you play will help, provided you emphasise number one. This emphasis need only be a gentle one. In fact, if you are concentrating correctly on the accented beat, you will find that the accent will happen naturally. In all of those examples, once you have mastered the required movements you should keep repeating the rhythm until it becomes light, brisk and dance-like. (Examples 9, 10, 11, 12, 13).

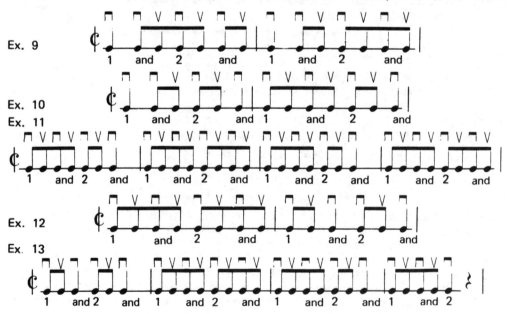

Ex. 9

Ex. 10

Ex. 11

Ex. 12

Ex. 13

9

To give you an idea how these rhythms might be used in context here is an extract from a flute and bodhrán duet.

Ex. 14   Transcription from a flute and bodhrán recording made in Quilty, Co. Clare in 1979 with J. P. Downes, flute, and Marcus Walsh, bodhrán.

It is now time for you to start experimenting yourself, if you have not done so already. In the absence of a willing victim to accompany, any good recording of Irish traditional music will serve the purpose. Select at this stage a reel or a hornpipe. If you do not already play a traditional instrument, learn to hum or lilt the melody you wish to accompany. Concentrate initially on keeping in time with the basic pulse, then gradually begin to alter your rhythms to fit in with the spirit of the tune. Accompanying a solo instrument is probably best, particularly a solo flute. Even though you will not be using technically complex strokes at this point, good bodhrán playing rests far more on the player's ability to produce a vibrant, precise and 'lifting' sound at this technical level.

## THE DOUBLE DOWN-STROKE

We now come to the element which distinguishes the double-ended stick style from the other styles and methods. What we have been practising up to now is known in traditional terminology as 'singling the beat'. The double-down stroke is used in 'doubling the beat' in this style.

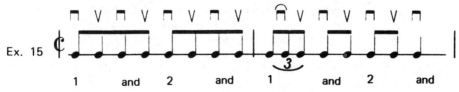

Ex. 15

1      and      2      and      1      and      2      and

The double down-stroke is shown here by the symbol ⊓ placed over the first two notes of a triplet. The third note is played with an up-stroke and illustration 9 explains the full movement.

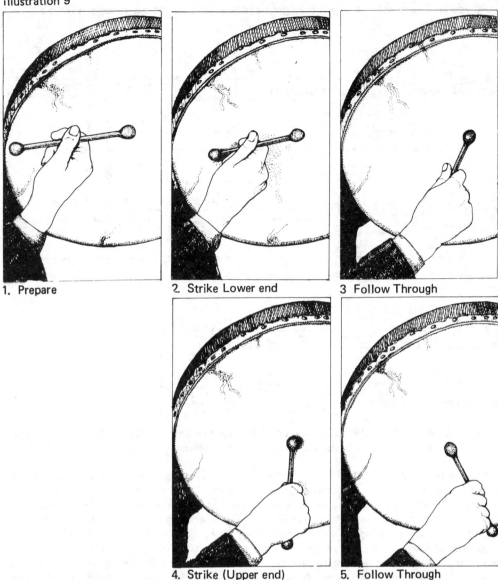

1. Prepare     2. Strike Lower end     3 Follow Through

4. Strike (Upper end)     5. Follow Through

The easiest and most natural way is to let it happen itself. The idea of random play is important here again. Begin by playing a regular series of beats at a moderate speed (Example 16).

Ex. 16

Now, start to relax your grip on the stick very gradually until it is almost at the point of slipping out of your hand. The top end of the stick will begin to rotate wildly. By maintaining just enough pressure to prevent the stick from slipping between your fingers, and by maintaining a steady beat with the lower stick end, you will find that the upper end will begin to fly in occasionally to hit the skin. When this happens you have produced a double down-stroke. Learning to control this is the next step.

Go back to the regular series of even beats shown in Example 16 but this time playing at a slow careful speed. Keep a firm but not a tense grip on the stick. Now, whenever you want a double down-stroke, increase the swivel of the stick almost as far as it will go. If the top end of the stick is not hitting the skin at this stage, it probably means that there is too much of an angle between skin and stick. You can reduce this angle by altering the stick position or by inclining the bodhrán itself in towards the stick.

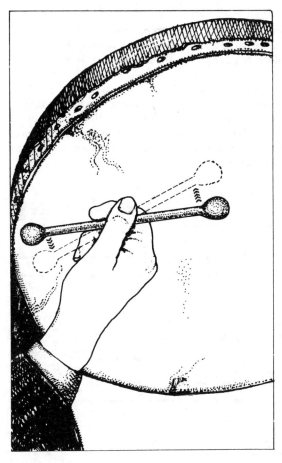

10a    Reducing the Angle

10b    Inclining the Bodhrán

Try to play a double down-stroke on the first beat of each bar. Begin by 'singling the beat' and gradually attempt to introduce the 'doubling' effect. If at times it doesn't happen when you intend it to, or vice versa, keep playing without breaking the rhythms and try again when you have steadied the beat. For 'doubling' to be natural, it should grow out of the 'singling' movement which must be maintained constantly.

Ex. 17

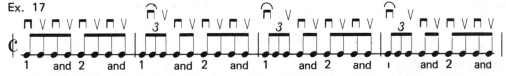

1    and 2    and 1    and 2    and 1    and 2    and 1    and 2    and

The essential feature of the double down-stroke is that the regular swivelling motion of the stick is not disturbed. Example 18 and Example 19 are produced, therefore, by the same wrist speed. It is the increased extent of stick rotation causing the top end of the stick to come into play, which 'doubles' the beat.

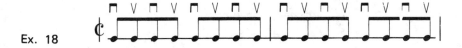

Ex. 18

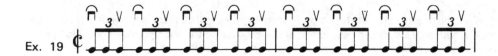

Ex. 19

There is no cause to worry if your double down-stroke is not happening exactly as shown in the illustrations. It probably only means that you are using one of many slight variations caused by the amount of arm movement from the shoulder as opposed to the use only of arm rotations from the elbow.

You should now experiment some more, this time mixing the various strokes to produce varied rhythms. Hum, lilt or whistle a reel or hornpipe and try to feel where the double down-strokes might best suit. In actual performance, you should curb the natural inclination to over-do the double down-stroke. Also, don't neglect the use of the 'silent up-stroke' mentioned earlier. This provides a welcome relief to the ear and counteracts the obvious danger of a monotonous barrage of sound. Example 20 shows the double-down stroke in context.

Ex. 20     Transcription from a flute and bodhrán recording made in Quilty, Co. Clare in 1979 with J. P. Downes, flute, and Marcus Walsh, bodhrán.

## THE DOUBLE JIG

All rhythms up to now have been suitable for accompanying reels. The same technique will also produce rhythms for hornpipes, single jigs, polkas, marches and some slip jigs. Double jigs, most slip jigs and slides, being in compound time, require a different approach. Those who do not read music can learn to identify the different tune-types by listening to suitable recordings. The basic beat for the double jig is in Example 21.

Ex. 21

13

There are three ways of playing this on the bodhrán, depending on the order of down-strokes and up-strokes.

Ex. 22

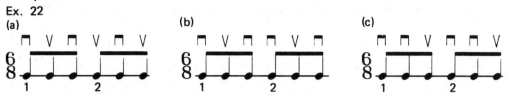

Each method produces an individual sound characterised by the slight variations in accentuation which are caused by the different locations of the down-strokes. There is no need to confine yourself to any one method. Learning to mix them at will is not only a good discipline but will also allow you greater flexibility when it comes to using double down-strokes. The reason for this is because it is only by a combination of methods that down-strokes can be played on any one of the six beats. Practise the following:

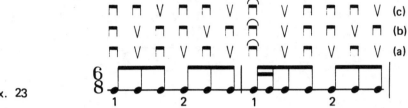

Ex. 23

By trying all methods for a while, you will find one which appeals to you most. In all cases, the difficulty lies in manipulating the up and down movements of the stick in order to place a down-stroke or double down-stroke where you want it. In the following examples, the player should follow his own style, although other approaches have been suggested in some cases.

Ex. 24

Ex. 25

Ex. 26

Ex. 27

14

In the case of the slip jig, there are two approaches each following the two types of that jig.

Ex. 28A

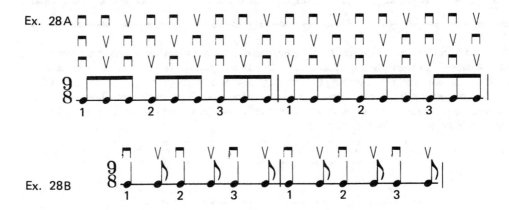

Ex. 28B

Practise the following rhythms:

Ex. 29

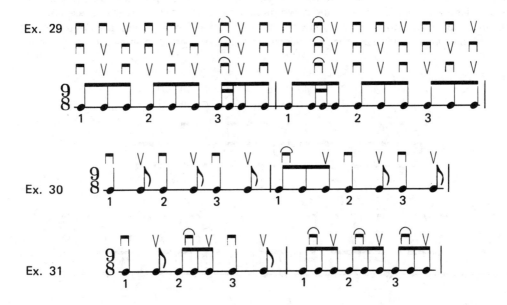

Ex. 30

Ex. 31

The technique used in type B Slip Jigs is also used in single jigs as in the following examples:

Ex. 32

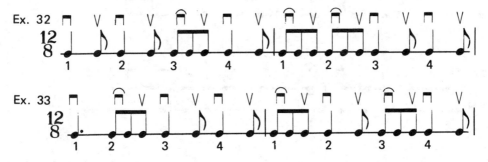

Ex. 33

15

# 3. other playing methods

## SINGLE ENDED STICK-STYLE

The essential feature of this style is the practice of 'doubling' with one end of the stick rather than with both ends. A popular way of holding the stick in this style is to grip it at one end between the thumb and forefinger. Players in this style sometimes use a stick with a knob at the playing end only. Others use a double knobbed stick with the unused knob resting against the palm of the hand.

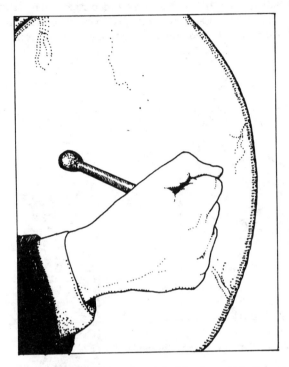

Illustration 11    Holding the stick (single ended stick-style)

'Singling' is achieved in the same way as for the double ended stick-style. There is, however, a different quality of sound apparent and greater volume is possible. 'Doubling' may be obtained in a number of ways. The most direct is to double the speed of arm rotation to produce a fast down-up-down movement of the stick. This is not as difficult as it first seems on account of the increased length of stick between the hand-grip and the playing point.
(Example 34).

Ex. 34

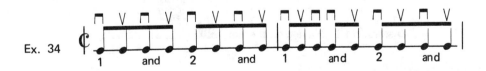

1    and    2    and    1    and    2    and

Part of the distinctiveness of this style is the urgency and staccato nature of the 'doubling' effect. The extra physical effort required conveys itself through the rhythm.
(Example 35).

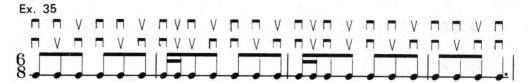

Depending on factors like the tension of the skin, other methods of 'doubling' may be used. In these cases, the stick is allowed to rebound off the skin to produce two beats with the same stick end, either on a down or an up movement. The effect is more like a short drum-roll than the precise beats of the other methods. Experimentation will find the method most suitable for you. Another method of holding the stick in the single ended stick-style is shown in illustration 13. A very short stick of about 3" is used here, with a knob at one end and a leather thong fastened to the other. The forefinger is slipped through the thong and the hand closed like a loose fist.

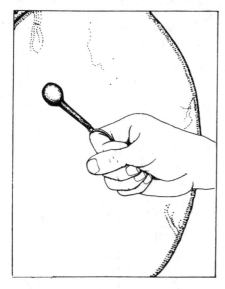

Illustration 12    Another method of holding the stick

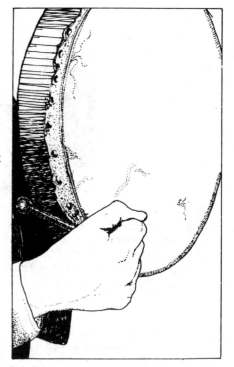

Illustration 13    Playing on the rim

## PLAYING ON THE RIM

One of the advantages of the single ended stick-style is that all the techniques of skin-playing can be transferred to rim-playing, even with a narrow rim. The double down-stroke of the other stick-style demands more space for the use of both ends of the stick, and as a result 'doubling' can be difficult at times. Playing on the rim has fallen out of fashion with younger players, but it was widely practised among the older generation.

Rim-playing is usually done at the start of a tune part and continued until the end of that part where the player reverts to skin-playing. The reason for this is, to allow the player to take advantage of the breathing space at the end of most tune parts (eight bar sections) when the bodhrán rim can be turned towards the stick without a noticeable break in rhythm.

## THE HAND STYLE

Most hand technique is the same as that used in the single ended stick-style except for the question of rebounding on the skin in some strokes. In hand-playing this is not really practicable. Rim-playing without a stick is, of course, not practised. The main advantage in hand playing seems to lie in the particular quality of sound. Setting the skin vibrating with the hand can produce a richer *timbre*, less brittle than that caused by the stick. The usual way of shaping the hand is shown in Illustration 14. The same form of arm rotation is used as in the other styles and the drumskin is struck with the backs of the fingers.

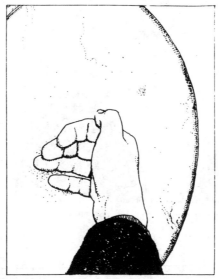

Illustration 14   Shaping the hand

'Doubling' is obtained by the same fast hand-movement described on pages 16 and 17.

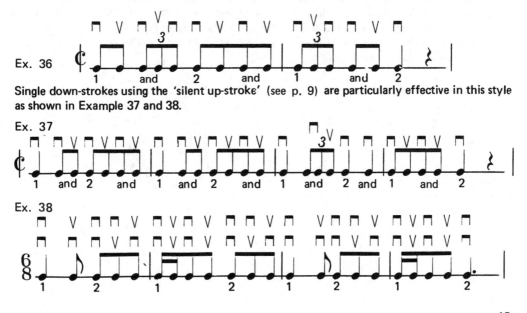

Single down-strokes using the 'silent up-stroke' (see p. 9) are particularly effective in this style as shown in Example 37 and 38.

A second means of shaping the hand is to make a fist. The index finger is now pointed out straight and the thumb automatically finds a comfortable resting place. Turn the hand around from the wrist in the usual fashion until the index finger is pointing at your chest. The only part of the hand to strike the skin is the back of the Index finger.

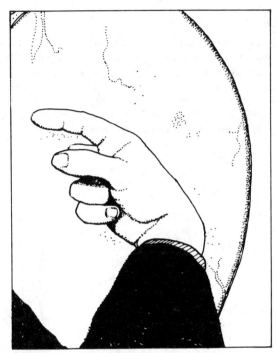

Illustration 15   Another method of shaping the hand

## THE THUMB ROLL

This technique is also used in playing the orchestral tambourine. It is never used by today's younger bodhrán players and is quite rare among older performers. Found in hand-playing styles only it is associated with instruments which have jingles in the rim.

The thumb is extended from the fist and its tip is rubbed up against the skin. Provided the thumb is rigid, it will bounce rapidly along the skin causing a series of continuous beats like a drum roll. The hand movement should be swift and should have begun a little before the tip of the thumb makes contact with the skin. You can practise this on a table top by wetting the thumb first to help increase friction.

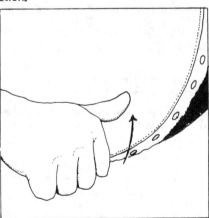

Illustration 16   Thumb Roll

# 4. contemporary developments

A brief word about new techniques will show how complex bodhrán performance has become. All of the developments outlined have been introduced since 1970 and are confined at present to a small number of professional bodhrán players mostly operating with traditional music groups.

## THE RIM SHOT

While playing directly on the rim is not favoured by younger players, a new form of rim playing has developed. The rim-edge over which the skin is stretched is used in such a way as to allow for a close mixing of skin and wood sounds.

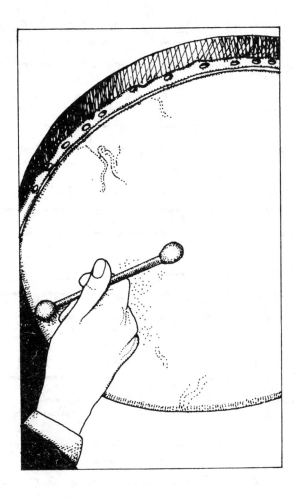

In Example 39 rim-shots are shown by the signs ⒭ or ⑂ depending on whether it involves a down-stroke or up-stroke.

Ex. 39   An extract from a bodhrán solo by Johnny McDonagh
         Recorded in 1980

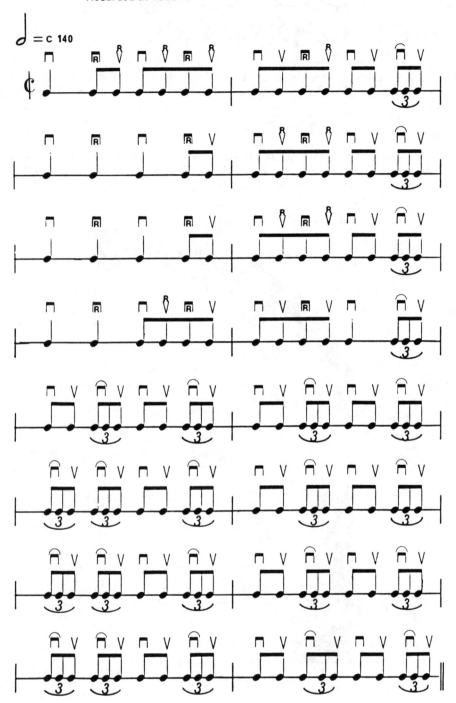

## RHYTHMS

A greater use of 'doubling' and of what might be called 'trebling' is to be seen in Example 40. 'Trebling' involves a further subdivision of the beat by increasing the arm-rotation speed.

Ex. 40    An extract from a bodhrán solo by Tommy Hayes
          Recorded in 1980

## USING THE LEFT HAND

Balancing the bodhrán on the knee while sitting and supporting it with the back of the left hand resting against the cross-piece has allowed the left-hand free to involve itself with actual playing. There are three forms of left-hand usage.

a)    *Dampening the skin:*    This was not unknown among older players but it is now very widely used to effect the dynamic level of sound. Full dampening, by placing the left-palm flat against the inside of the skin, produces a dry sound. Variations of this are performed by using one or more fingers instead of the full palm. The effect is also dependent on the point of the skin which is struck by the right hand.

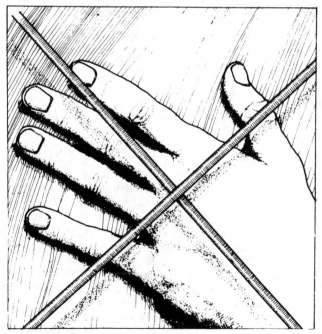

Illustration 18    Dampening the Skin

22

b)    *Altering the skin-tension:* This is achieved by pressing one or more fingers of the left hand in against the skin. The subsequent increase in skin-tension causes the pitch to rise. There is, of course, a certain dampening of sound as well. A subtle use of this technique has opened up a new dimension of possibilities in bodhrán playing.

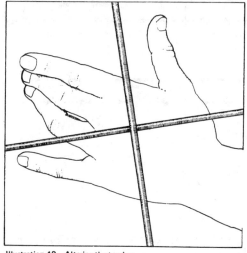

Illustration 19    Altering the tension

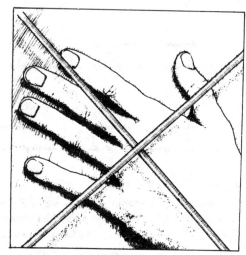

Illustration 20    Slapping

c) *Slapping*

The use of the left-hand directly for sound production is involved here. With the heel of that hand against the inside of the skin, the palm and fingers are swung in to slap the skin. Its usual use is to emphasis certain beats being played by the right hand.

Ex. 41    In this transcription of an example of slapping as performed by Tommy Hayes (recorded in 1980), the notes with down-stems denote slapping points.

Right Hand

Left Hand

## SYNCHRONISATION

Certain detailed forms of 'tune-following' are obtained by pre-arrangement between the bodhrán-player and the musician or musicians he is accompanying. This technique has arisen in connection with traditional music groups rehearsing pieces for their concerts and can range from the synchronisation of a change of meter (e.g. a sudden change from a double-jig into a reel) to the bodhrán player following the general melodic outline of the tune. This latter effect is done by altering the skin-tension with the left hand as already described.

In Example 41, the falling pitch of the melody is followed on bodhrán by beginning with the highest skin tension and by relaxing the left-hand slowly to bring down the pitch. It is more a question of following the melodic contour rather than following the precise pitches of the melody. Similarly, my notation system in this case involves the use of a three-line stave with the lowest line representing the Bodhrán skin in its normal unaltered tension, and the highest line representing the highest skin tension.

Finally, a few words on what we might term 'bodhrán etiquette'! Sensitivity of a social as well as of a purely musical kind is demanded of the player today. Playing with friends at a private

23

session is probably the best situation for 'letting go'. In a more public session, however, where the bodhrán sits in with seasoned players, playing 'out of turn' is an insensitivity of the highest order. Unless you are a competent player, able at the very least to synchronise with the basic pulse of the music while controlling the volume of sound, it is far better to maintain a wise silence.

The bodhrán is both the easiest of the traditional instruments to join in at a session with, and also potentially the loudest. The combination of both factors often spells disaster for the other musicians who are either forced to eject the bodhrán-player, or else disband the session and move somewhere else without telling him!

Ex. 42    An extract from a performance by Maurice Lennon, fiddle, and Tommy Hayes, bodhrán, (both of the group Stockton's Wing) recorded in 1980. Hayes has developed a personal technical style which is not covered by the Bodhrán notation in this book. Symbols are therefore omitted from this extract and also from Examples 40 and 41. The title of the tune is 'Tripping down the Stairs'.

25